T0004624

WHO WOULD WIN?

ULTIMATE OCEAN RUMBLE

BY
JERRY PALLOTTA

ILLUSTRATED BY
ROB BOLSTER

Scholastic Inc.

16-CREATURE BRACKET

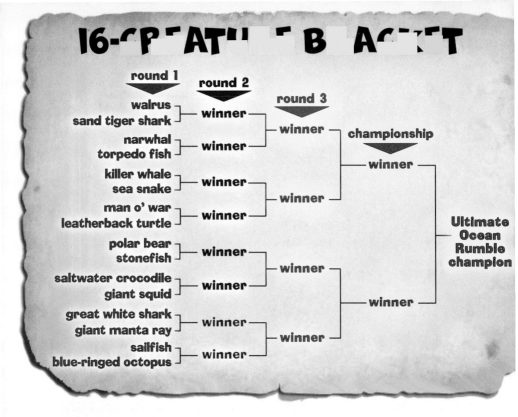

round 1

round 2

round 3

championship

walrus
sand tiger shark — winner
narwhal
torpedo fish — winner
— winner
killer whale
sea snake — winner
man o' war
leatherback turtle — winner
— winner
polar bear
stonefish — winner
saltwater crocodile
giant squid — winner
— winner
great white shark
giant manta ray — winner
sailfish
blue-ringed octopus — winner
— winner

winner

winner

winner

winner

winner

Ultimate Ocean Rumble champion

Thank you #21, Malcolm Butler of the University of West Alabama.
—*J.P.*

To my friend Santiago of Westwood. The old man and the sea.
—*R.B.*

Text copyright © 2015 by Jerry Pallotta.
Illustrations copyright © 2015 by Rob Bolster.

ISBN 978-0-545-68118-6

40 39   23 24

Printed in the U.S.A.   40
First printing, September 2015

Book design by Rob Bolster

Sixteen sea creatures have agreed to participate in a bracketed battle. The first round has eight matches. It's single elimination. If a creature loses, it is out of the competition. Our first match is walrus versus sand tiger shark.

ROUND 1

WALRUS VS. SAND TIGER SHARK

MATCH 1

As soon as the walrus gets off the ice, it will face the hungry shark.

SAND TIGER WINS!

The walrus jumps off the ice floe and tries to outswim the sand tiger. The shark catches up and bites a flipper. Ouch!

FACT
The only seal bigger than a walrus is the elephant seal.

DID YOU KNOW?
Walrus skin is 3 to 4 inches thick.

The walrus is badly hurt. Its blubber didn't protect it. The sand tiger shark wins.

The second match in round one features a narwhal versus a torpedo fish. Who would win if they had a fight?

FACT
The long tusk of the narwhal is actually an overgrown tooth.

DID YOU KNOW?
A narwhal is an Arctic sea mammal that breathes air.

ROUND 1 — NARWHAL VS. TORPEDO FISH — MATCH 2

The torpedo fish, also known as an electric ray, leaves the ocean bottom and swims toward the narwhal.

FACT
Most rays live close to the ocean floor.

SHOCKING FACT
The jolt of electricity from a torpedo fish is strong enough to kill a person.

NARWHAL WINS!

The torpedo fish attempts to give an electric shock to the narwhal. The intelligent narwhal scores a direct hit with its long, pointy tusk. Narwhal wins!

FACT
A narwhal also uses its long tusk to break breathing holes in ice.

ELECTRIC FACT
After giving a shock, the torpedo fish has to "recharge itself" to give another shock.

The narwhal will now move on to round two and come face-to-face with the sand tiger shark.

The third match has a killer whale against a sea snake.
The orca wants nothing to do with snakes. Snakes? Yuck!

DID YOU KNOW?
*A killer whale is also
known as an orca.*

WILD FACT
*Killer whales are always
black and white. Most live
in a group called a pod.*

FACT
*A killer whale that
does not belong to a pod
is called a rogue.*

ROUND 1 — KILLER WHALE VS. SEA SNAKE — MATCH 3

It doesn't look like a fair fight. A giant sea mammal
versus a skinny little reptile. Watch out, killer whale—
a deadly, poisonous snake!

DEFINITION
*Sea snakes have a tail
shaped like an oar.*

FUN FACT
*Sea snakes look like eels, but
they are not fish. They are
reptiles.*

KILLER WHALE WINS!

Wham! The killer whale doesn't fool around. It knows the sea snake carries deadly poison.

> **SWIMMING FACT**
> Sea snakes live in the ocean and come on land only to lay their eggs.

> **FACT**
> A sea snake can hold its breath for five hours.

> **DID YOU KNOW?**
> Orcas are considered the greatest predators on Earth.

The killer whale pins the snake and breaks its bones. The snake never saw it coming. The killer whale will be moving on to the next round.

Our fourth match in round one has a Portuguese man o' war facing off against a leatherback turtle.

FACT
A man o' war is not a jellyfish.

FUN FACT

The tentacles of a man o' war can reach more than 100 feet long.

IT'S TRUE

A man o' war is a siphonophore. That means it is actually made up of hundreds of smaller sea creatures.

ROUND 1 — MAN O' WAR VS. LEATHERBACK TURTLE — MATCH 4

This match showcases an excellent swimmer versus a drifter. The leatherback turtle's legs are like wings.

TWO FUN FACTS
Turtles are reptiles.
Turtles do not have teeth.

MAN O' WAR WINS!

The leatherback turtle is careless and swims into the stinging tentacles of the man o' war. The stinging poison gets in its eyes, nose, and throat. It proves to be deadly.

DRIFTING FACT
The man o' war drifts with wind, waves, currents, and tides.

BIG FACT
The leatherback turtle is the largest of all turtles. They can grow up to 7 feet long and weigh up to 2,000 pounds.

SWIM FACT
Leatherbacks are fast swimmers and can be found in all oceans.

FACT
Sea turtles come to the surface to breathe air.

STRANGE FACT
Leatherback turtles eat mostly jellyfish.

Sorry, turtle! The man o' war wins the match.

What is a polar bear doing in an ocean book? Polar bears are considered sea mammals. They live on the Arctic Ocean's ice.

DID YOU KNOW?
Polar bears are also called ice bears.

FACT
A polar bear can smell a seal from one mile away.

ROUND 1 — POLAR BEAR VS. STONEFISH — MATCH 5

At the shoreline, the polar bear takes a walk into the ocean. The bear doesn't know there is a stonefish patiently waiting for a fish dinner to swim by.

DID YOU KNOW?
Stonefish spikes can pierce a boot.

11

STONEFISH WINS!

The stonefish is camouflaged and looks like rocks on the bottom. Oops! The polar bear steps on the stonefish. Ouch! The stonefish's deadly poison will kill the polar bear.

GROSS FACT
Stonefish poison is a neurotoxin. It makes your muscles stop moving, and you can't breathe.

STRONG FACT
Polar bears are so strong they can drag a 2,000-pound dead walrus with their teeth.

DID YOU KNOW?
Polar bears are excellent swimmers. People have witnessed them swim more than 50 miles.

The ugly stonefish will move on to the second round, but who will it fight?

The next match is the one everyone has been waiting for. It's still the first round, match number six! Saltwater crocodile versus giant squid.

ROUND 1 — SALTWATER CROCODILE VS. GIANT SQUID — MATCH 6

The saltwater crocodile is an ambush predator. It patiently waits for the giant squid to swim nearby. The squid is looking for something to eat.

SALTWATER CROCODILE WINS!

The saltwater crocodile flaps its huge tail and attacks in a burst of energy. It grabs the squid and takes a huge bite. The giant squid shoots ink, but Saltie doesn't even notice.

ATTENTION!
An adult saltwater crocodile will eat any large animal, including humans!

The saltwater crocodile wins. It is off to the second round.

Finally! The world-famous great white shark has entered the tournament. It's match number seven! Great white shark versus giant manta ray.

HOLLYWOOD FACT
A great white shark starred in the movie Jaws.

GREAT WHITE SHARK VS. GIANT MANTA RAY

ROUND 1

MATCH 7

This fight is teeth, teeth, and more teeth versus a filter feeder. The giant manta ray is huge. Maybe it can smack the shark silly.

DID YOU KNOW?
Manta ray wings can be as long as 30 feet from wing tip to wing tip. That's longer than most private airplanes.

DEFINITION
A filter feeder is an ocean creature that eats by straining small food from the water.

FACT
A giant manta ray can jump completely out of the ocean.

GREAT WHITE SHARK WINS!

The fearless shark goes right at the giant manta ray and bites it in the face. The great white enjoys the meal.

SIZE FACT

The largest of all rays is a giant manta ray. They can weigh up to 3,000 pounds! That's a ton and a half.

SHARP FACT

Great white shark teeth are serrated, triangular, and as sharp as steak knives.

DID YOU KNOW?
Teeth are not bones.

The ferocious great white shark gets past round one. No one is surprised.

It's the last match of the first round. The sailfish meets up with a blue-ringed octopus.

ROUND 1 — SAILFISH VS. BLUE-RINGED OCTOPUS — MATCH 8

It's speed against poison! Fish versus mollusk!

BLUE-RINGED OCTOPUS WINS!

The sailfish leaves deep water and swims near the coral reef, looking for food. The blue-ringed octopus gets startled and jumps on the sailfish's back.

DID YOU KNOW?
A sailfish is a pelagic fish.

DEFINITION
A pelagic fish is not found in one place. It swims all over the world.

As the fish shifts into high gear, the octopus injects its venom. The sailfish is out of the tournament.

The first round is over. Do the math. The tournament began with sixteen creatures. Half are out, so divide sixteen by two. Only eight are left.

Ding! Ding! Ding! Round two has begun. Narwhal versus sand tiger shark.

ROUND 2 — NARWHAL VS. SAND TIGER SHARK — MATCH 1

A fish against a whale is a great matchup. The narwhal has to come up for air. The shark doesn't. Who has the advantage?

SAND TIGER SHARK WINS!

The narwhal and the sand tiger fight back and forth.

The long tusk prevents the narwhal from making fast turns. The narwhal is no match for the shark! The shark wins!

It's round two, match two. The killer whale swims over to meet up with the man o' war.

ROUND 2

KILLER WHALE VS. MAN O' WAR

MATCH 2

Uh-oh! Is this a trick? Not one but hundreds of man o' wars are in the water.

MAN O' WAR WINS!

The killer whale accidentally sucks a man o' war into its blowhole. The poison and stinging tentacles enter the killer whale's lungs.

WARNING! POISON!
Never ever touch a man o' war. It has deadly chemicals that can hurt humans.

DID YOU KNOW?
A killer whale is the largest of all dolphins.

FUN FACT
A killer whale has no natural enemies and is not an endangered species.

The killer whale is in big trouble. Its mouth, tongue, sinuses, and lungs are burning from the deadly man o' war chemicals. It withdraws from the competition. Sadly, the much-anticipated match between the killer whale and the saltwater crocodile is not going to happen. There is always next year!

Round two, match three! This time it is saltwater crocodile versus stonefish. If this was a beauty contest, no one would want a photo taken with either creature.

DID YOU KNOW?
There are more saltwater croc attacks worldwide every year than shark attacks.

SALTWATER CROC. VS. STONEFISH

GOOFY FACT
If this match was a movie, the title would be Saltie Meets Spikey.

The crocodile uses its tail to muddy the water. Now the stonefish can't see well. Where is that crocodile?

SALTWATER CROC WINS!

The crocodile uses a smart tactic. While the stonefish is motionless on the bottom of the ocean, the crocodile uses its three-foot-long jaws to bite the stonefish sideways. Crunch! The spines never touch the crocodile.

DEFENSIVE FACT
A saltwater crocodile is so ferocious that even a small one is dangerous to humans.

FACT
Crocodiles often bury their prey underwater to eat later when the meat is more tender.

The reptile has won. The stonefish is dead. Saltwater crocodile is going to the semifinals!

This is the last match in round two. Great white shark versus blue-ringed octopus. Everyone expects the great white shark to advance to the finals.

AIRBORNE FACT
A great white shark can jump completely out of the water.

ROUND 2 GREAT WHITE SHARK VS. BLUE-RINGED OCTOPUS MATCH 4

JET POWER
The blue-ringed octopus moves by pushing water out like a jet engine.

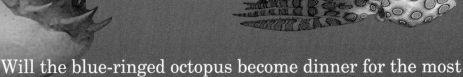

Will the blue-ringed octopus become dinner for the most feared shark in the ocean? Is the blue-ringed octopus afraid? Is the great white shark smart enough to avoid the poison?

The great white shark tries to swallow the blue-ringed octopus. But the shifty octopus doesn't get swallowed right away. It gets into the shark's gills.

One, two, three seconds, and the shark cannot shake the octopus. The octopus injects its deadly venom. The shark is losing consciousness. The great white shark stops swimming and sinks. It's not looking so "great."

The blue-ringed octopus moves on to the next round.

The second round is over. Should we call the next two matches the third round or the semifinals?

In basketball it's called the *Final Four*.
In ice hockey it's called the *Frozen Four*.
We now present the *Ocean Four*.

Wow! It's down to a siphonophore, a fish, a reptile, and a mollusk. The sea mammals can only watch.

 # MAN O' WAR VS. SAND TIGER SHARK

It's a sand tiger shark versus a man o' war. In baseball they might say "play ball!" We say, "May the best creature win!"

STRANGE FACT
The Ocean Four *are all cold-blooded animals.*

ANOTHER STRANGE FACT
Of the original sixteen sea creatures, the killer whale, walrus, narwhal, and polar bear are warm-blooded animals.

SAND TIGER SHARK WINS!

The sand tiger shark flicks its tail and breaks the man o' war into pieces. The shark gets stung, but it shakes it off. The shark has toothlike skin. The man o' war gets caught in a current and washes up on the beach.

TOOTH FACT
The hard, rough "teeth" on a shark's skin are called denticles.

The sun's heat kills the beached man o' war. Watch out! Even dead, it's still poisonous. Don't ever touch one. The sand tiger shark moves on to the finals.

And now the other half of the *Ocean Four*! Saltwater crocodile versus blue-ringed octopus. Saltie has defeated the giant squid and the stonefish.

SALTWATER CROC VS. BLUE-RINGED OCTOPUS

The octopus has already defeated the sailfish and the great white shark. Saltie is not fooling around. It heads straight for the blue-ringed octopus. Beware of its poison!

SALTWATER CROC WINS!

Chomp! In one lightning-fast bite the saltwater crocodile chops the blue-ringed octopus in two! The octopus didn't have time to figure out how to bite a reptile that weighs 1,000 times more than itself.

WEIGHT FACT
A saltwater crocodile can weigh up to 2,000 pounds. That's a ton!

WEIGHT FACT
A blue-ringed octopus weighs only two pounds.

DISTANCE FACT
Scientists tagged a saltie and recorded it swimming 600 miles in open ocean.

Poison is a great weapon, but this time it didn't help. The nasty saltwater crocodile is heading to the finals!

It's the final match of the tournament. Sand tiger shark versus saltwater crocodile. Can the rugged shark beat the nastiest reptile on Earth?

BEWARE!
Most shark attacks happen at dusk, in estuaries or in cloudy water.

CHAMPIONSHIP MATCH!

PAY ATTENTION!
Most saltwater crocodile attacks occur near the shoreline or in crocodile-infested lagoons.

The smaller sand tiger shark is too timid for the huge, ferocious saltwater crocodile.

SALTWATER CROC WINS!

The crocodile positions itself just right and delivers a fatal bite to the shark. It's over! The biggest, meanest reptile on Earth wins! The saltwater crocodile wins the Ultimate Ocean Rumble.

This is one way the competition might have ended. How would you rewrite the brackets?